PULLING MUSSELS

About the author
Nic Outterside was an award-winning newspaper journalist and editor for 28 years and currently is the proprietor of *Time is an Ocean*, the book publishing arm of **write**_ahead_. *Pulling Mussels* is his thirty-eighth paperback book.

PULLING MUSSELS

Nic Outterside

Time is an Ocean Publications

Time is an Ocean Publications
An Imprint of **write***ahead*
Lonsdale Road
Wolverhampton, WV3 0DY

First Printed Edition written and published
by **Time is an Ocean Publications 2021**
Text copyright © **Nic Outterside**
The right of Nic Outterside to be identified as the author of
this work has been asserted by him, in accordance with the
Copyright, Designs and Patents Act 1988.
The front and back cover photographs are
copyright © **Time is an Ocean**
All images within this book are copyright
© **Time is an Ocean** except where
the individual copyright of the owners are accredited.

All rights reserved.
This book is sold subject to the condition that it shall not, by way of trade
or otherwise, be lent, hired out or otherwise circulated in any form of
binding or cover other than that in which it is published. No part of this
publication may be reproduced, stored in a retrieval system, or transmitted
in any form or by any means (electronic, mechanical, photocopying,
recording or otherwise) without the prior written permission of
write*ahead*.

DEDICATION

For Eric's children Pamela, Jacqueline,
Anne and Roderick
And for his 10 grandchildren and many
more great grandchildren

Contents

FOREWORD	PAGE 1
THE STORY	PAGE 3
Chapter 1 Born In Time	PAGE 4
Chapter 2 Flying Sorcery	PAGE 10
Chapter 3 Brave New World	PAGE 17
Chapter 4 Bells of War	PAGE 23
Chapter 5 Back and Forth	PAGE 33
Chapter 6 Post World War Two Blues	PAGE 39
Chapter 7 Swinging Through the Sixties	PAGE 47
Chapter 8 The Autumn of Their Lives	PAGE 52
Chapter 9 Death is Not the End	PAGE 57

THE POETRY	PAGE 63
ACKNOWLEDGMENTS	PAGE 94
PICTURE CREDITS	PAGE 95
ABOUT THE AUTHOR	PAGE 97

Foreword

We build our legacy piece by piece, and maybe the whole world will remember you or maybe just a couple of people, but you do what you can to make sure you're still around after you're gone.

David Lowery (writer and filmmaker)

Eric Charles Pounsett was a remarkable and unique man for so many different reasons.

He was born illegitimately to a poor servant girl in an age where both mother and son would normally end up in the workhouse. Yet both were helped and protected by one of the wealthiest families in England.

At five years old he met and shook hands with the first man to fly the English Channel and by 1970 was the only person alive to tell of such an experience.

At 12 years old, during World War One, he was used as *"ballast"* in a Royal Flying Corps test flight of a new biplane.

From the age of 13 he chain-smoked 60 cigarettes a day and somehow managed to wheeze himself to the age of 75.

He left school at 14 and by his own admission was uneducated, yet he became a published poet with many of his poems printed in newspapers and read out on national radio.

He helped create a multi-national refrigeration business, resigned his directorship after an argument with his friend the MD. He then returned six years later to see the company become a world-famous brand.

He was christened *Mr Shoreham*, after his adopted home town of Shoreham by Sea, by famous BBC broadcaster and entertainer Charlie Chester.

He made and lost several small fortunes, once owned three shops, and died almost penniless in a West Sussex psychiatric hospital.

But much more than all of that, he was a loving husband and father to four children… and he was my grandfather.

This book has been more than 40 years in the making and I am truly sorry that it wasn't written or published while all of Eric's children were still alive.

This is his story, plus a selection of some of his quirky and timeless poetry.

Nic Outterside
November 2021

ERIC CHARLES POUNSETT
1904-1979
THE STORY

Chapter One
Born in Time

When tiny Eric Charles Eastman was born on a wild and wet Wednesday in a dingy farm labourer's cottage in rural Hampshire, few could have imagined how his incredible life would unfold over the next 75 years.

The facts that Eric would never know his real father and that the storm that swelled around him was *"the worst in living memory"* added an extra poignancy to the moment he entered this world on 3rd February 1904.

Eric's mother Lucy Ann Eastman

His mother was 28-year-old Lucy Ann Eastman, a spritely and attractive young woman used to manual agricultural graft as much as she was to skilled dressmaking with fine silk and a seamstress needle.

Indeed, after leaving school aged 15 and to better her chances in life, Lucy had gone into service as a maid in two wealthy homes in London.

At the turn of the century some 1.5 million people in England were employed as live-in domestic servants for the wealthier classes.

5 Portland Place, Marylebone

In 1898, Lucy became a parlour maid for Percy and Rachel Marsden and their daughters 16-year-old May and 17-year-old Vera at their imposing five-storey Georgian house at 5 Portland Place, Marylebone.

This incredibly wealthy family also owned the even grander Eaton House in up-market Belgravia.

At their Portland Place address, the Marsdens had a staff of nine live-in servants including a domestic butler, a cook, two parlour maids, two house maids, a kitchen maid, a scullery maid and a lady's maid.

After the cook and butler, Lucy was third in seniority among the staff. It was indeed an age of Upstairs/Downstairs and a rigid class system of rich and poor.

Today (2021) single apartments at this sought-after address (renumbered to 28 Portland Place after the devastation of the area by German bombing in World War Two) now sell for between £4 and £5 million each!

Even at the end of the 19th century, Portland Place was a highly desirable address for senior Hampstead stockbroker Percy Montagu

Moses Marsden and his family who were also leading philanthropists in the London Jewish community.

Percy's cousin was the renowned British writer Ada Leverson, a friend of Oscar Wilde, who had cared for him after he was released on bail at the height of the national scandal surrounding Wilde's homosexuality.

However, the move into service with the Marsdens was to prove to be both Lucy's undoing and her salvation. By all accounts Lucy quickly became a close and trusted member of the Marsden family.

But in the late spring of 1903 disaster struck.

Following a passionate and illicit affair with the family butler, Lucy found out she was pregnant. The identity of the butler was to remain anonymous to everyone for the next 118 years – all Lucy would say, in later life, was that *"he was just the butler"*.

But now thanks to internet family search engines and a DNA analysis, I can reveal that the butler in question was a 43-year-old Lancastrian man named Thomas Bowker – some 15 years Lucy's senior.

Having initially identified Thomas as the most likely butler and "father" from national census records and the DNA analysis, I found that as Eric's grandson, I shared DNA matches and chromosome strands with five members of the immediate Bowker family tree.

According to the 1891 census, Thomas was living at an address in Queen Street near Southwark Bridge in London with his wife Margaret and baby daughter Evelyn-May.

But, by 1901 Margaret had moved to Sellincourt Road in Streatham in a poorer quarter of South-East London. There she listed Thomas as her husband who was *"sleeping away"* from home at 5 Portland Place, Marylebone.

By this time the couple had five children: Evelyn-May now 11 years old, Violet aged 8, Lela aged 6, Lulu aged 3 and one-year-old Constance.

Meanwhile, in 1903 Lucy's pregnancy was both a serious and pressing problem.

It could have been concealed by the wealthy household with her immediate marriage to the butler. But of course, Thomas was already married with children of his own – although they were living with his wife some eight miles away.

So, marriage was out of the question.

This was the makings of a social scandal for the Marsdens and devastation for Lucy. For a working-class woman to have a baby out of wedlock in Edwardian times was a guaranteed fast route to the workhouse, starvation and public ridicule.

We don't know how Thomas was dealt with by the Marsden family, but in 1904 he was no longer in their employment. He then moved back north to Lancaster where he died three years later in 1907, aged just 47 years old.

But we do know the Marsden family all wrapped themselves around Lucy to protect her during the first few months of her pregnancy and paid her as she continued to do light duties for the household.

Then sometime in late autumn 1903, Lucy returned to her parent's cottage at Enham Estate near St Mary Bourne, a village between Whitchurch and Andover in the rural environs of north Hampshire.

We don't know the exact date of her return, but we know that the Marsdens provided one of their best horse-drawn carriages to take her home to the protection of her family.

Once back home, Lucy was cared for by her mother Mary and farm labourer father William who helped prepare quietly for the birth of her child.

But when it was time to give birth, poor Lucy couldn't have chosen a worse day.

On Wednesday 3rd February, with rain lashing down outside and water finding any leaks in the cottage roof, the whole country was hit by a terrible storm with widespread flooding and high winds.

Indeed, a freak tidal wave swept along the east coast of England from the North Sea and into the English Channel. Many coastal villages and much farmland in Kent, Sussex and Hampshire were flooded.

Although people fled as the wave hit the coasts, many were also drowned. In East Anglia the tidal wave washed across the low-lying land ruining hundreds of acres of flower bulbs and potato crops.

7

It was heralded in the press at the time as *"the worst storm in living memory"*.

The Eastman's cottage at Enham, near St Mary Bourne in Hampshire where Eric was born

Eric couldn't have had a more startling entry into this world.

His birth, and his christening nine days later 12th February – we presume at the parish church of St Peter in St Mary Bourne – were both registered some years later at the Lambeth registry office in London.

Although the start of World War One was still 10 years away, the world that Eric was born into was already moving fast.

King Edward VII had acceded Queen Victoria on the British throne just three years prior to Eric's birth and the country was governed by Arthur Balfour and his Conservative cabinet.

In January 1904, number plates were introduced for motor cars, which were being licensed for the first time and a national speed limit of 20 miles per hour was instated. The popular *Daily Mirror* had been launched as a daily morning pictorial newspaper using photographs for the first time. And a month after Eric's birth, Britain's first surface electric trains began running from Liverpool to nearby Southport.

In May that year Charles Rolls and Henry Royce met for the first time, at the new Midland Hotel, Manchester, to agree production of Rolls-Royce motor cars. And in November, Finchley fire brigade in north London became the first to take delivery of a petrol-engined self-propelled motor fire pump.

But probably more significant is the UK was the signing of the Entente Cordiale with France – a political agreement, which in 1914 would drag the world into war.

Others to share Eric's birth year were photographer Cecil Beaton, actors Cary Grant and Sir John Gielgud, entertainer George Formby, author Graham Greene, MP and Founder of the Open University Jennie Lee and England cricketer Harold Larwood.

This was Edwardian England at the start of the 20th century.

Chapter Two
Flying Sorcery

Baby Eric was cosseted and cared for by his doting mother and grandparents plus uncles George, Henry and Walter, who all lived nearby and did the odd bit of babysitting.

Life was a rural routine centred around planting, milking, harvests and hard work, with no NHS and no safety net of unemployment pay or incapacity benefits.

Although Lucy must have hankered to return to a more comfortable life in London, her first duty was to raise her son.

But things were to change again in 1906, when she met and fell in love with travelling seed salesman Stephen Edwin Pounsett from rural Epping in North London.

Stephen Pounsett circa 1900

Tall and erudite, at 29 years old Stephen was a year Lucy's junior and already had plans to better his life by training to be a printer and journalist.

It wasn't long before the educated Stephen not only proposed to marry Lucy, but to take her back to London and be a father to two-year-old Eric.

With financial help – we believe from the Marsdens – Lucy acquired a small, terraced house in Felden Street in Fulham, not far from Eel Brook Common and Parsons Green.

This was her registered address, when on 30th March 1907, she and Stephen were married at St Peter's Church, Fulham, just a stone's throw from her new home. The wedding witnesses were Lucy's brother Walter and his wife Kate.

St Peter's Church, Fulham after being bombed in World War Two

Sadly, St Peter's Church – and the terraced housing around it - was badly damaged by German bombing in World War Two and demolished at the end of the war. Today only grainy photographs of its original structure remain.

A short while after their wedding, in the early autumn of 1907, Stephen moved his new family south to the Kent coast. As the sole breadwinner his days as a humble printer had paid off and he had secured a job as Printer's Overseer (head of the print room) with the daily newspaper the Dover Express and East Kent News.

The Pounsetts moved into a modest terraced house at the top end of St James Street, just south-west of Dover Castle.

The move held a fortuitous irony.

Across the channel in France, engineer Louis Blériot had designed a monoplane that managed to fly 17 miles from Toury to Ateny on 31st October 1908, setting a world record for distance flown. Two weeks before that, on 16th October, former US cowboy Samuel Cody made the first powered flight in the British Isles. Together, these two events led the daily newspaper the *Daily Mail* to offer a £1,000 prize (worth about £122,000 by today's values) to the first person to cross the English Channel in a *"heavier-than-air"* machine.

The summer of 1909 saw two serious contenders, Louis Blériot and Hubert Latham, who were both waiting in France for unseasonable windy summer weather to abate.

At about 2.30am on the morning of Sunday 25th July, Blériot was driven to Barraques, near Sangatte. There he was to make his Channel attempt in his Blériot No XI 25-horsepower monoplane.

The machine was made of ash and poplar and strengthened with piano wires. The controlled parts were the wings, the elevator that took the place of a tail and a rudder that also acted as a balancing fin. It had a Chauviere propeller, and it was powered by a three-cylinder Anzani motorbike engine.

Dawn was breaking but it was still quite windy when at 4.40am, Blériot set off.

One of his aides immediately sent a signal to the Lord Warden Hotel in Dover's Pier District, where reporters from the *Daily Mail* were staying.

Blériot's wife, Alice, was on board the French destroyer Escopette that was to follow Blériot across the Channel and, if there was an accident, to rescue him.

About halfway across the strait, Blériot ran into a bank of cloud. Although he did have a compass on board the wind blew him off course to the east.

When the cloud cleared, he saw what he believed to be the South Foreland and followed the coast west to the pre-determined landing site at Northfall Meadow – 300 metres northeast of Dover's Castle and less than a mile from Eric's home in St James Street.

This spot had been chosen by one of Blériot's aides as the cliffs are relatively low and the engine was too weak to bank and climb far. He landed at Dover 36 minutes 30 seconds after take-off, travelled at an average speed of 42mph at an altitude of 250ft.

A small crowd – among them young Eric Pounsett – greet Louis Blériot

Due to the gusty wind conditions, Blériot had switched the engine off before landing and so bumped to earth. This caused damage to the undercarriage and shattered a propeller blade.

There were two French journalists, one of whom had been primed to fly the French Tricolour flag from the chosen landing spot waiting to greet him.

V Ker Seymer – a Royal Aero Club official – was on site to verify the flight; Police Constable John Stanford and a few soldiers, who were on duty at the time, were there to meet him.

News of the feat quickly spread and among those already there alongside the *Daily Mail* photographers were 32-year-old local newspaper man Stephen Pounsett and his five-year-old stepson Eric.

Many years later in 1972, Eric had a letter titled *The Day I shook Louis Blériot's Hand* published in the *Shoreham Herald* in which he detailed his memories of the day:

"On 25th July 1909, in the Northfall Meadow, near Dover Castle, I shook the hand of Louis Blériot," he wrote.

"My father, who was with the Dover Express and East Kent News had brought me along to watch the arrival of the first aircraft to fly the 22 miles across the English Channel.

"I can still remember seeing that speck on the horizon and hearing the excitement in my father's voice, cheering that chugging frail aircraft on, as it came just over the cliff top heading for Whitfield, the landing field.

"I remember the wind in the valley below the castle catching the aircraft and forcing it to land into the side of the hill, damaging its under carriage and one wing.

"Bleriot climbed out of his exposed seat little the worse for wear for his rough landing.

"Very few people witnessed Blériot's arrival. I was only five and half years old and I wonder how many other people who are still alive today were there for that amazing historical moment.

"What marvels we of this century have lived through. Just think, man on the moon is already inside page news and Concorde no longer excites. Yet 63 years ago Blériot made world history" he added.

The day after the first cross channel flight, Dover's Mayor, Walter Emden, in honour of Louis and Alice Blériot, gave a civic luncheon at the grand 110 bedroom Lord Warden Hotel. It was attended by Stephen, Lucy and Eric Pounsett.

Many VIPs had stayed at the Lord Warden Hotel over the years including, in March 1871, Napoleon III, Emperor of France, who was reunited with his wife Empress Eugenie and son after his release from Wilhelmshole Castle, Germany. Charles Dickens frequently stayed at the hotel and in a letter dated 1863, he made reference to the nearby streets which provided the atmosphere in his novel *Bleak House*. George Eliot was another regular customer who famously stayed in 1854 while waiting for her lover George Lewes. So, it was indeed a prestigious venue to celebrate Blériot's success.

A civic reception was held to celebrate Blériot's flight at the Lord Warden Hotel. Among the crowd were Stephen, Lucy and Eric Pounsett

A granite memorial to commemorate his landing on Northfall Meadow was later laid in 1910.

Alexander Duckham of Duckhams Oil, who was involved in the building of the Admiralty Harbour at the time, paid for the Monument. The granite is believed to belong to the same batches as used in the construction of the harbour.

During all the hype and celebrations, Gordon Selfridge, proprietor of the famous department store, was motoring around Kent. On hearing of the historic flight, he made an appointment to see Blériot and persuaded the pioneer to exhibit his craft at his Oxford Street store. Following the exhibition, the plane was returned to Paris.

The achievement brought not only fame for Blériot but it also changed people's attitude towards flying, and by the end of the year, Blériot's factory in France had orders for over 100 aircraft. He continued to design and produce new planes and his business expanded accordingly, producing fighter aircraft during World War One.

Stephen and Lucy Pounsett's young family became settled in Dover and as Eric grew he became as active member of the local Boy Scout troop and his pre-occupation with flying machines knew no bounds!

In 1972, he further reminisced in the *Shoreham Herald*: *"Blériot was the first, but there were so many other pioneers,"* he wrote.

"I can still remember a number of them making their test flights from the airfield just west of Dover Castle. Such frail skin and bone machines powered by 25hp engines that could not even take off if there was a breeze blowing.

"Some even ran on wooden rails laid along the ground, the end of which sloped upwards to assist take off.

"I also remember the Silver Queen and The Beatle, two of the early Dirigibles (air ships) that visited Dover."

When World War One broke out in 1914, 10-year-old Eric helped the war effort as a Boy Scout cyclist messenger taking communications between military bases along the local Kent coast.

"During the war, the same airfield where I had witnessed some of the early pioneering flights were used by the Royal Flying Corps and the American Air Force," he later wrote.

"It was there when I went for my first flight in, if I remember correctly, a BE 9 (an experimental recognisance bi-plane). It was a two-seater open cockpit.

"I was a 12-year-old Boy Scout stationed at the airfield and was smuggled on board as ballast by a young pilot on a training flight. He had to have a passenger in his cockpit for weight and balance reasons and could not find a colleague that keen on flying off duty hours."

When World War One ended in November 1918, Eric was 14 years old and although a bright student – good at English and mathematics – it was time for him to leave school and try to carve out a career in his chosen line as an electrician.

Chapter Three
Brave New World

With a new post war world ahead of everyone, Stephen and Lucy decided it was also time to search for better pay and prospects.

So, in 1919-1920 the whole family returned to London and moved into a modest terraced home at 298 Fulham Road in West Brompton.

Britain had enjoyed an economic boom in the immediate post war years as private capital pent up over four years of war was invested into the economy.

The shipbuilding industry was flooded with orders to replace lost shipping (7.9 million tons worth of merchant shipping stock was destroyed during the war).

However, by 1920, the transition from a wartime to a peacetime economy faltered, and a serious recession struck the whole country after 1920. With other major economies also mired in recession, the export-dependent economy of Britain was particularly hard-hit. Unemployment reached 17% in 1924, with overall exports at only half of their pre-war levels.

So, with job prospects bleak, young Eric began to train as an electrician while Stephen luckily found a better paid job in a newspaper print room in Fleet Street.

Lucy, meanwhile, became a Lady's companion and dressmaker for the Duncan Earl of Camperdown's household in plush Charles Street – a road of embassies and consulates, where today buildings often exchange for £50 to £80 million a time.

She developed a fine taste in clothes and would often be given cast off gowns and extravagant dresses as gifts for her service. She would also gain a taste for fine foods and wine - a far cry from the peasant stew and wood pigeon broth her mother used to cook.

It seems she had obtained this comfortable position due to sparkling references from the Marsden family.

Eric (centre) working on a refrigeration contract at Harrods in 1925

In 1925, Eric turned 21 and while undergoing his apprenticeship servicing freezers at the prestigious department store Harrods in nearby South Kensington, he met the love of his life: a bubbly and attractive Chelsea girl named Ruby Florence Langham.

Ruby was the second youngest child of 11, of ship's carpenter Alexander Langham and his wife Charlotte.

She was also 21 and worked in the wages and counting house of Harrods, where Eric would leave her short love poems every lunch time.

Ruby lived with her parents in Arthur Street near St Luke's Church in Chelsea, a short bus ride from Eric's family in West Brompton.

The couple became inseparable and well before Christmas 1925 Eric proposed marriage to Ruby. As New Year 1926 dawned it was to become a pivotal time in both their lives. In January, Eric and Ruby were married at Chelsea Registry Office.

But then came a huge shock. Before the wedding banns could be read, Eric had to obtain his birth certificate. Lucy said she didn't have one.

Then while applying for the certificate, the registrar at the Lambeth registration district office called him to one side to explain why the certificate was so brief and irregular.

It was then Eric saw that his name on the certificate was Eric Charles Eastman and not Eric Charles Pounsett and to complicate matters there was no name of any father.

It didn't take long for the penny to drop.

One can imagine the shock that reverberated inside him to first discover that his beloved dad Stephen was not his natural father and secondly that he was born illegitimately!

Many years later Ruby recalled: *"We were both shaken to the core as we had always assumed that Stephen Pounsett was his father.*

A copy of Eric's birth certificate as it was presented to him in 1926

"Eric was in shock for many days and needed lots of support and also a promise that I would never reveal the details of his birth certificate to anyone.

"He felt total shame… yet none of this was his fault – and carried that shame around with him for years.

"After Stephen died in 1956, he asked his mother Lucy who his real father was, but she said he didn't need to know because Stephen had been a proper father to him."

Many years later, when in her dotage Lucy confided to Ruby: *"His dad was just the butler where I worked."*

Back in 1926, following their pre-marital shock and with their first child on the way, Eric and Ruby settled down to married life and a house at 16 Fawcett Street, West Brompton – less than half a mile from Eric's previous address in Fulham Road.

Then with electrician jobs at a premium, Eric managed to find employment with upmarket department store and food retailer Fortnum and Mason as a delivery driver at their Piccadilly headquarters.

But as ever, good luck was tempered by bad.

On a cold April morning while Eric was trying to crank start his delivery van, the engine rotors snapped back the iron starting handle which then flipped over and broke the main radius bone in Eric's right forearm. He was hospitalised and ordered to rest while the bone was re-set and healed.

But history was about to overtake Eric's life when a month later a national General Strike was called.

The strike lasted just nine days, from 4th to 12th May 1926. Some 1.7 million workers across the country went out on strike, especially in transport and heavy industry. It was called by the General Council of the Trades Union Congress (TUC) in an unsuccessful attempt to force the British government to act to prevent wage reductions and worsening conditions for locked-out coal miners.

In the meantime, the government put in place a militia of special constables called the Organisation for the Maintenance of Supplies (OMS) of volunteers to maintain order in the street.

One special volunteer constable said afterwards: *"It was not difficult to understand the strikers' attitude toward us. After a few days I found my sympathy with them rather than with the employers.*

"For one thing, I had never realized the appalling poverty which existed. If I had been aware of all the facts, I should not have joined up as a special constable."

For Eric the strike was a disaster. And to add insult to injury, his employer Fortnum and Mason assumed that because Eric was not at work, then he must have been on strike. He was summarily sacked from his job, with no recall or appeal. Added to that, his arm never healed properly and remained awkwardly bent for the rest of his life.

But 22-year-old Eric was a born fighter and on 29th May 1926 - less than three weeks after losing his job - he obtained his first driving licence and was determined to pursue his dream career as an electrical engineer. And with his first child Pamela born at St Mary's Hospital, Paddington in July 1926, steady work and a regular pay packet was a priority for the young Pounsett family.

Eric successfully finished his apprenticeship and in 1928 had secured a job as a trained electrical engineer with US refrigeration firm Frigidaire.

In 1928 US company Frigidaire gave Eric his first big break

Frigidaire was founded as the Guardian Frigerator Company in Fort Wayne, Indiana, and developed the first self-contained refrigerator in 1916 and later the first home food freezer. In 1918, William Durant, a founder of General Motors, personally invested in the company and in 1919, it adopted the name Frigidaire. The brand was so well known in the refrigeration field in the early-to-mid-1900s, that many Americans called any refrigerator a Frigidaire regardless of brand. In France, Canada, and some other French-speaking countries, the word Frigidaire is often in use as a synonym today, while in the UK it is simply shortened to Fridge.

In the 1920s electric fridges were not yet mass-produced and were mainly owned by the very wealthy.

As the cost started to drop, the market expanded. Worldwide sales rose from 200,000 in 1926 to 1.5 million in 1933. By the mid-1930s, the number grew to around six million. By the time Eric joined them as a young electrical engineer in 1928 Frigidaire were undisputed world leaders in refrigeration setting the pace for the decade to come.

When his second child Jacqueline was born in St George's Hospital, Fulham in January 1931, Eric was an experienced and qualified refrigeration engineer servicing fridges and freezers for wealthy clients and upmarket retail stores.

Chapter Four
Bells of War

In 1933 came the break that Eric was waiting for when Frigidaire moved its star electrical engineer to front up its operation in Sussex.

In June that year, Eric, Ruby, Pamela and toddler Jacqueline moved from their small Fawcett Street home in West Brompton to a new house at 10 Brookfield Villas on the Brighton Road in South Lancing - near Shoreham Airport in an area known as Widewater.

Businessman Eric in 1938

"They are some of my earliest memories," said Jacqueline.

"Brookfield Villas were lovely and dad built us a little play house cottage in the back garden. He was a brilliant dad, always making us things or writing poems," she added.

"Dad also had a silver Frigidaire delivery van and a telephone... to have a motor vehicle and a phone in those days was unheard of for people of our class.

"We must have stood out among our neighbours, but we soon made friends and got on with all of them so well.

"There wasn't any jealousy… dad worked damn hard to provide for us and everyone was helping each other as most families had raw memories of the recession and the unemployment of the previous decade.

"It also seems that Frigidaire must have thought highly of dad to equip him so well," she added.

A delivery van similar to the one Eric drove in the 1930s

For the first time in their lives Eric and his family were devoid of money worries and sent their older daughter Pamela to fee paying private school Erringham Girls Public Day School, initially at 25 Rosslyn Road, Shoreham before moving to 18 Buckingham Road in 1937. The school's principal was a Mrs Sybil Reed.

Within three years, Frigidaire bonuses were rolling in. Eric had developed his patch along the Sussex coast and was servicing and selling fridges and freezers for clients as diverse as Fred Batten's dairy in Shoreham, Bonetti's ice creams in Worthing and wet fish merchant Charlie Purley in Bognor Regis.

By 1936, Eric was highly experienced and ready to go solo with his own business as a refrigeration engineer and salesman.

In the autumn of that year the family moved less than a hundred yards along the road and bought a retail showroom which Eric named *Refrigeration House*, complete with a large flat above.

Although strictly speaking the new address was still Lancing, the only thing separating the Pounsett's home and business from Shoreham were a few fields and the Norfolk Bridge.

Brighton Road, Lancing adjacent to Eric's Refrigeration House

Eric's experience, contacts and charm seemed to work as most of his Frigidaire clients followed him to his new independent business. Fridge and freezer sales boomed. His family also grew with the birth of a third daughter Anne in 1935 and son Roderick in 1939.

But then world events again took over when World War Two was declared on 3rd September 1939.

Upon the declaration of war some 70,000 UK resident Germans and Austrians became classed as enemy aliens.

By 28th September, the Aliens Department of the Home Office had set up internment tribunals throughout the country headed by government officials and local representatives, to examine every UK registered enemy alien over the age of 16. The object was to divide the aliens into three categories: Category A, to be interned; Category B, to be exempt from internment but subject to restrictions and Category C, to be exempt from both internment and restrictions.

By February 1940, nearly all the tribunals had completed their work assessing some 73,000 cases. The vast majority (some 66,000) of enemy aliens being classed as Category C. Some 6,700 were classified as Category B and 569 as A. Those classified in Category A were interned in camps being set up across the UK.

However, by May 1940, with the risk of German invasion high a further 8,000 Germans and Austrians resident in the south of England, found themselves interned.

Resident Italians were also considered for internment following Italy's declaration of war on Britain on 10th June 1940.

With many of his local Italian ice cream vendors interned for the duration of the war, Eric's refrigeration business collapsed in the summer of 1940.

But the outbreak of war had another and quite different impact on Eric and his family.

When France fell with such rapid speed in June 1940, just six weeks after the German invasion, along with the ensuing evacuation of British forces from Dunkirk, all eyes were on what Hitler would do next.

Britain, although apparently defeated, exposed and isolated, did not surrender. It did not even seek to come to terms with Germany.

The Germans now had two options: to lay siege to Britain and to wear it down physically and psychologically through limited military action and propaganda warfare, which would include the threat or bluff of invasion; or to actually invade.

So, on 16th July 1940 Adolf Hitler issued Directive Number 16. It read: *"As England, in spite of the hopelessness of her military position, has so far shown herself unwilling to come to any compromise, I have decided to begin to prepare for, and if necessary to carry out, an invasion of England... and if necessary the island will be occupied."*

But the Germans, surprised by the speed of their military success in Europe, had no detailed plans for an invasion.

This absence of a plan did not prevent Hitler from announcing that an invasion force would be ready to sail by 15th August. The operation was given the codeword Sealion.

Hitler hoped that when the British realised what was coming their way, their will to resist would crumble.

26

From mid-July the Luftwaffe stepped up the military pressure by attacking the channel ports and shipping to try and establish command of the Straits of Dover, while German heavy guns were installed around Calais to bombard the Dover area.

But by the end of July neither the threat of imminent invasion nor offers by Germany of honourable peace had done the trick. It appeared that Germany would actually have to execute one of the most difficult military operations imaginable: an invasion, launched across at least 20 miles of sea, culminating in a landing on a fortified and desperately defended coastline.

A gun emplacement on Worthing seafront in 1940

On the last day of July, Hitler held a meeting where he was told by his generals of the difficulty in obtaining barges suitable to carry invasion troops and the problems of massing troops and equipment.

The German navy meanwhile argued for the invasion front to be reduced from the proposed 200 mile beachhead (from Lyme Regis in the west to Ramsgate in the east) and for a postponement of the invasion until May 1941.

Hitler rejected these requests and instead postponed his planned invasion to 16th September. He decided that the Luftwaffe should tighten the screw by attempting to clear the channel of British warships and the skies over southeast England of British aircraft.

Shoreham Beach after all the bungalows were demolished to make way for war defences

Meanwhile in Britain everyone was having to guess what Hitler's plans might be. Anti-invasion defences of all types had been planned and executed with incredible speed since late May. At the same time, a new force had been organised to help defend the country.

The Local Defence Volunteers (LDV) was raised on 14th May 1940 and comprised men too old or too infirm to join the regular army or in protected trades and thus exempt from conscription. On 23rd July, it became known as the Home Guard.

By the end of July one and a half million men had volunteered, a huge figure which reveals the seriousness with which ordinary people took the threat of invasion in the summer of 1940.

And the call went out that if an invasion did begin then church bells across the south of England would ring out signalling for everyone to mobilise and where possible vulnerable people and children to move inland.

The Kent and Sussex coast was to offer a series of barriers or stop-lines formed by concrete pillboxes, gun emplacements, antitank obstacles, trench systems, minefields and barbed wire entanglements and utilising natural and man-made features such as rivers, canals and railway embankments. They were to ensnare and delay the German forces.

But the Luftwaffe assault on the RAF began to go awry as Goering changed the emphasis of attack from radar stations and airfields to aircraft factories and more peripheral targets - thus giving RAF front line squadrons a much-needed breathing space.

While what became known as the Battle of Britain started to reach its crescendo, the debate about Operation Sealion also continued to rage between the German navy and the army.

Eventually a compromise was reached. On 13th August, Hitler agreed that the invasion front should be narrowed, with the most westerly landing area being around Shoreham and Worthing.

This meant that the only one German Army Group - Army Group A - would carry out the invasion.

The attack group of the German 9th Army was to leave from Le Havre and land in the Brighton-Worthing area of Sussex. The first assault wave was to secure the beachhead.

The second wave was made up of two Panzer Divisions - each composed of tanks, artillery, mobile troops and Panzer grenadier assault infantry - and one motorised division.

These landings were to be supported by parachute troops, who were to drop on the Downs above Brighton and Shoreham, to assist in the securing of the beach head for the Brighton-Worthing assault group.

But the day after he had agreed a narrower invasion front Hitler told his generals that he would not attempt to invade Britain if the task seemed too dangerous. There were, said Hitler, other ways of defeating Britain.

As Hitler started to back away from invasion the battle for dominance of the skies over England and the English Channel - a battle that now, perhaps, had little strategic value - reached a new peak of fury.

A Messerschmidt ME109 brought down at Shoreham Airport in 1940

On 3rd September, with the RAF still far from destroyed, Field Marshal Keitel, head of the Armed Forces High Command, delayed Sealion until 21st September, and then again until 27th September, the last time the tides would be right before the end of the year.

The day after this last postponement was announced, Goering launched his final major offensive to destroy RAF Fighter Command in daylight action. It was a dismal failure, with the Luftwaffe losing twice as many aircraft as its victim.

On 17th September - two days after Goering's defeat - Operation Sealion was postponed indefinitely. The plan was never to be revived. Hitler's attention was drawn increasingly to the east, and in June 1941 he invaded the Soviet Union.

Back home in Shoreham the Territorial Army gunners 113th Regiment of Field Artillery based in Worthing set up a field Headquarters at Buckingham Park.

The guns, 25 pounders, were dug in at Buckingham Park and were ranged onto the airport and Shoreham Beach where it was thought the invasion landings might occur.

The National Service Act was introduced and call up was announced for all men between the ages of 18 and 40. Close to the older age limit, 36-year-old Eric wanted to volunteer but his family persuaded him that he was of greater service at home.

Meanwhile, street lighting was turned off, the black-out introduced, cars had hoods with slits fitted over their headlights. Road signs were taken down to confuse any invading armies and white lines were painted on roadways, black and white kerb stones fitted onto pavements.

Access to and from Shoreham Beach via the footbridge was only permitted at certain times. There was a curfew and residents had to be home by 9 o'clock when the footbridge was closed, the middle section drawn back to prevent access and a guard posted at Kings Drive at the road entrance to the Beach.

Most of the bungalows and old railway carriages that were built into them were blown up by the Army from West Beach to Ferry Road and all along the foreshore right up to the Old Fort.

Large containers of a mixture of petrol and oil were installed in the grounds of Caius School, now Shoreham College, at Kingston. Pipelines ran underground to more fuel tanks at the harbour mouth and canal ready to be pumped out and set on fire by the Navy in the event of invasion.

The residents of Bungalow Town had to evacuate homes in a hurry and leave most of their furniture behind.

A line of defensive obstructions and concrete blocks were placed all along the open stretches of coastline. Beaches were mined, barbed wire entanglements set up and gun emplacements were made along the riverbank by the airfield, and two large Bofors anti-aircraft guns sited in the Nicolson Drive end of the Ham Field allotments.

Gas attacks were a real fear and gas masks were issued to everyone young and old. At school children were shown how to wear the gas mask and ensure that it was carried at all times.

The members of the ARP (Air Raid Precautions) patrolled the street at night and warned residents of any lights which were showing with the call *"put that light out."* Each member carried a whistle which they were to blow when warning of a gas attack or unexploded bomb in the vicinity.

The ARP was based with the Fire Brigade at their HQ in the old school in Ham Road. This combined team were trained to deal with bombings, fires and provide first aid. Important buildings like the post office and the town hall were sandbagged to reduce damage from bomb blasts.

Air raid shelters were built in Ham Road, another was in Connaught Avenue on the green and behind Victoria Road School as well as many others strategically placed around town.

And so, during the summer and autumn of 1940 began a large and often uncoordinated evacuation of vulnerable adults and children from Kent and Sussex.

And wrapped up in this whole melee was Eric and his young family.

Eric had already volunteered to be an ARP warden long before the war began and his ARP card from Worthing Rural District Council is dated 11th January 1939 and addressed to Refrigeration House on Brighton Road, Lancing.

"Dad was so keen to join up and fight long before the war," said his daughter Jacqueline.

"But fearing a German invasion and with a young family in tow, mum wanted him back at home.

"And at 35 years old he was on the cusp of an older age group who would be put in the army reserves and not directly sent to fight," she added.

"So being an ARP warden was the least he felt he could do."

And in the summer of 1940, the whole family's evacuation from the Sussex coast was only a matter of time.

Chapter Five
Back and Forth

In July, Eric and his family moved lock, stock and barrel to a new home in Willesden in North London to be close to Eric and Ruby's families.

Eric secured a job in nearby North Kensington with Sunbeam Talbot, who built upmarket sports-saloon cars.

During the war years the company built its prestige cars and parts for aero engines from its plant at Barlby Road.

Eric and his family rented a terraced house in Doyle Gardens adjacent to King Edward VII Park in south Willesden and settled down to London life. And as war raged around them Eric took up his ARP duties with a new vigour.

But while any planned German troop invasion of the Sussex coast had failed to materialise, in September 1940, Hitler suddenly turned his attack on the British capital. The Luftwaffe had lost the Battle of Britain and the German air fleets (Luftflotten) were ordered to attack London, to draw RAF Fighter Command into a battle of annihilation.

From 7th September 1940, London was systematically bombed by the Luftwaffe for 56 of the following 57 days and nights in an operation which became known as the Blitz. Most notable was a large daylight attack against London on 15th September. Large air battles broke out, lasting for most of the day. The first attack merely damaged the rail network for three days, and the second attack failed altogether. The air battle was later commemorated by Battle of Britain Day. The Luftwaffe lost 18 percent of the bombers sent on the operations that day and failed to gain air superiority.

While Göring was optimistic the Luftwaffe could prevail, Hitler was not. In the last days of the battle, the bombers became lures to draw the RAF into combat with German fighters.

The Luftwaffe gradually decreased daylight operations in favour of night attacks and the Blitz became a night bombing campaign after October 1940.

The first deliberate air raids on London were mainly aimed at the Port of London, causing severe damage. The change in strategy caught the RAF off guard and caused extensive damage and civilian casualties. Some 107,400 gross tons of shipping was damaged in the Thames Estuary and 400 people were killed.

Eric on duty as an ARP warden in London, with field telephone

The Germans round-the-clock bombing of London was an attempt to force the British government to capitulate, but it was also striking at Britain's vital sea communications to achieve a victory through siege.

On 14th October, the heaviest night attack to date saw 380 German bombers from Luftflotte 3 squadron hit London. Around 200 people were killed and another 2,000 injured. British anti-aircraft defences fired 8,326 rounds but shot down only two bombers.

The next day, the bombers returned and about 900 fires were started by a mix of 376 tons of high explosives and 10 short tons of incendiaries dropped. Five main rail lines were cut in London and rolling stock damaged.

The operation carried out by the 10th Air Corps concentrated on delayed action parachute mining operations against shipping and civilian and industrial areas. By 20th April 1941, it had dropped 3,984 mines. The mines' ability to destroy entire streets earned them fear and respect in Britain.

A German parachute mine with timing device similar to the one dropped adjacent to the Pounsett's home in 1941

American observer Ralph Ingersoll reported the bombing was inaccurate and did not hit targets of military value but destroyed the surrounding areas.

More than 40,000 civilians were killed by Luftwaffe bombing during the war, almost half of them in the capital, where more than a million houses were destroyed or damaged. The so-called parachute mines, with their delayed action fuses were deadly and many had obliterated entire streets across London.

Then in April 1941, a mine was dropped onto Herbert Gardens which ran parallel to the Pounsett's home in Doyle Gardens, and Eric decided it was time to re-evacuate his family back to the safer environs of rural Sussex. Only a few weeks earlier Ruby's 73-year-old mother Charlotte had been killed when a German bomb made a direct hit on her house in nearby Chelsea.

London was now too dangerous for families to stay.

Eric and Ruby with their young family in the back garden of their home in Lancing in 1944

Ruby and the four children were speedily moved to a small cottage in the village of Birdham close to Chichester Harbour and a few months later formally evacuated by the government to 10 Irene Avenue in Lancing to allow Pamela, Jacqueline and Anne to continue their schooling.

Eric, meanwhile, stayed in Willesden working at Sunbeam-Talbot during the day and carrying out dangerous ARP duties at night.

But long hours working with little sleep, and a diet of caffeine and Shippam's fish paste sandwiches took its toll. 37-year-old Eric suddenly collapsed with a severe glandular and throat infection. Whether his chain-smoking Craven A high tar cigarettes made things worse, we can only guess. He was taken to an isolation hospital amid fears he might have diphtheria and ordered to rest.

Thankfully it wasn't the highly contagious and deadly disease but an infection due to being exhausted and run down.

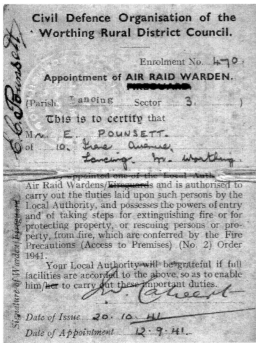

Eric's new ARP warrant card for Lancing

By the end of August, Eric was back in Sussex with his family in Irene Avenue and on 12th September 1941 he was appointed as an ARP warden for Lancing Sector 3. A month later he secured work at a government armaments factory sited at the Metal Box factory in Gardner Road, Southwick. Eric would cycle the five miles to and from work each day to help make 4MB artillery shells for the army. Then as before, he would undertake his ARP duties every night.

Although a lot safer than Blitz-hit London, the Lancing to Southwick area was by no means safe from the war, which by 1941-1942 had entered its bloodiest phase.

A total of 37 raids were carried out on Lancing, Shoreham and Southwick by enemy aircraft during the war. These involved 143 high explosive bombs, five oil bombs and in excess of 2,000 incendiaries causing the deaths of 17 people and injuring 108 others. Eight of these fatalities were local residents.

The worst death toll occurred on 21st October 1940 when a delayed action fused bomb landed by the Shoreham Shipping Company south of Brighton Road killed five people. Three others were killed and six injured in another attack on 9th November making eight Shoreham fatalities in total for the whole of the war.

The biggest raid of all was an attack on the railway bridge at Kingston Lane on the 8th October 1940 when 24 high explosive bombs were dropped and although they missed their mark, one hit the Church of St Michael at Southwick and resident Alice Ford was killed.

Shoreham airport received its fair share of attention from enemy raids. The airport's biggest raid of all occurred on 13th February 1943 when the control tower was hit and other building set on fire but otherwise no significant damage was incurred.

Then on 28th May 1944 German bombs killed nine ATS girls and one gunner in an attack on the army camp north of Lancing.

A German V1 flying bomb (Doodlebug) narrowly missed Lancing Chapel when it came down on 13th July 1944.

When VE day was celebrated on 8th May 1945, the war of attrition, blood, bombs and bullets against Nazi Germany and its axis allies Austria and Italy had lasted almost six years.

And like most others it had taken its toll on Eric and his family.

Chapter Six
Post World War Two Blues

The years immediately following the war were tough on everyone.

Not only was rationing to persist for another 11 years, but the whole country needed rebuilding. The war had stripped Britain of virtually all its foreign financial resources, and the country had built up sterling credits - debts owed to other countries that would have to be paid in foreign currencies - amounting to several billion pounds. Moreover, the economy was in disarray.

Some industries, such as aircraft manufacturing, were far larger than was now needed, while others, such as railways and coal mines, were desperately short of new equipment and in bad repair.

With nothing to export, Britain had no way to pay for imports or even for food.

To make matters worse, within a few weeks of the surrender of Japan, on 2nd September 1945, US President Harry S Truman ended lend-lease, upon which Britain had depended for its necessities as well as its arms during the war years. In international terms, Britain was bankrupt and although there was much work to be done, there was little to pay the millions of willing workers.

Eric, like most others, was looking for work and now aged 42 he was willing to move to wherever work could be found. Meanwhile, his former refrigeration client, friend and fish salesman Charlie Purley was becoming a bit of an entrepreneur himself.

In 1942, with his brother Frank Purley, Charlie who was 10 years Eric's junior, opened a factory for war work at Longford Road in Bognor Regis. Their company Longford Engineering Company continued producing munitions for the Admiralty and the War Office for the duration of the war.

Then in 1945, and with still a prime interest in keeping their fish fresh, the Purleys began making experimental refrigerators and in 1946 produced their first commercially available fridge from a new factory site on Shripney Road in Bognor.

By sheer chance Eric applied for the job of sales manager for Charlie's new company and with his expertise and experience in refrigeration engineering he was not only given the job, but also immediately promoted to sales director just before their mass production of fridges started at the beginning of 1947.

It also became a bit of a family affair in 1948, when Eric's daughter Jacqueline became the receptionist for the firm and lifelong friends with Charlie's daughter Joan.

Jacqueline also took on babysitting duties for Charlie Purley's small son David, who would later become a Formula One motor racing champion. He also became a national hero and was awarded the George Medal for his efforts to try to save his friend and racing colleague Roger Williamson who died in an horrific fire at the 1973 Dutch Grand Prix.

Meanwhile, back in post-war Sussex, Eric was enjoying success with the development and sales of fridges from the new Longford Engineering Company factory and in 1948 made history by overseeing the first consignment of fridges ever to be flown from England to Jersey in the Channel Islands.

The success of the venture helped open up direct trade with Belgium, the Netherlands and other western European countries.

By the end of 1949 the company was exporting refrigerators to Persia (now Iran), Iraq, Africa, India, Palestine, Spain, Norway and Iceland. Such was the success of the Bognor company that in the hard-pressed post war years some 50% of its output was for export consumption. And the man behind this success was Eric Pounsett.

But amid this fast-growing company and a raft of new employees and managers, tensions developed. Charlie Purley's robust and often confrontational style of leadership ruffled a few feathers. And his explosive and public outbursts with managers who he viewed were not performing as he wanted added to the work tensions.

Ever the gentleman, Eric was upset by Charlie's style of man management and in early 1950 resigned in protest as a director at Longford Engineering.

Eric (far left) oversees the first consignment of fridges to be flown to Jersey

With his three daughters now adults, ever the entrepreneur Eric set up and ran three shops in West Sussex including a pet shop, an ironmongers and a refrigeration business - the last with his new son-in-law Rick Turner – later co-owner of Turner and Keene TV and electricals in Steyning and Lancing.

Meanwhile, Longford Engineering was continuing to grow and changed its name to a snappier sounding LEC Refrigeration on 13th December 1954. By this time around 60% of its products were for the domestic market, with the rest for commercial use, but the company continued its strong export business.

LEC had a strong production base at its Shripney Works, a 14-acre site at Bersted next to the Bognor Regis branch railway line. On the other side of the railway, it had 56 acres of land, part of which was used as its own airfield to allow direct flights and exports of its fridges to customers in Europe and beyond.

The LEC production factory and airfield

In 1956, the company's principal pilot George Farley completed 1,000 hours of incident free flying with LEC, covering 120,000 miles. He crossed the English Channel 142 times and visited 23 countries including a business tour of 7,000 miles to the Middle East

Then another quirk of fate occurred in September 1956 when 52-year-old Eric was unexpectedly invited back to LEC to head up the company's prestigious showroom in Regent Street in the centre of London.

His return was heralded in the company's annual report and magazine at the end of the year where Charlie wrote: *"Eric was the Sales Director of Longford Engineering from 1945 to 1950. Many people will remember him. In those days contact between directors and other personnel was more intimate than it is now. So, we asked Mr Pounsett to give us an indication of how he felt about coming back to LEC after an absence of six years."*

Eric responded through the pages of the magazine: *"The developments that have taken place during the past six years at LEC are indeed most impressive.*

"The thing that impressed me more than the new methods, buildings and machinery was the number of familiar faces. A large percentage of the people who started at Longford Road are still with the company, and the keenness they have maintained through the years is astonishing."

And showing there was no lasting animosity between himself and Charlie Purley, he went on to say: *"Over the past six years I have remained in the friendliest association and contact with LEC and its directors. During which time I have been an agent and a service engineer for the company.*

"Our Regent Street showrooms are now fitted up with spectacular Christmas displays. LEC products are in keeping with the most prosperous shopping street in the metropolis and we belong there."

Ruby at the door of their cottage in Queen's Place, Shoreham

Eric's rollercoaster life had indeed reached a new peak as the 1950s decade ran to the end of its course.

By 1960, only 13% of homes in the United Kingdom had a refrigerator, compared to 96% in the United States. Around that time LEC produced its *Twelve Six* range of fridges, costing £179 each.

In 1958 Eric and Ruby acquired a new home, a terraced flint cottage at 19 Queen's Place in Shoreham and settled into a more home-loving life with their four children and 10 grandchildren all living nearby.

And LEC continued to grow. In 1970, the Co-op decided to produce its own range of freezers, manufactured by LEC, which retailed at £93. Throughout the 1970s, its freezers were among the *Which?* magazine's best buys.

By the beginning of the 1980s, it had around 1,600 employees, and had around 20% of the domestic refrigeration market in the United Kingdom. By the 1980s, the company was known as LEC Refrigeration plc, an LSE listed company.

LEC fridges and freezers still sell well today and are the go-to option in the medical profession and pharmacies throughout the UK. Indeed, during the Covid pandemic in 2020-2021 they were the first choice of fridge by Boots the Chemist to store the Covid vaccines.

One of Eric's exclusive photos of the scaffolding collapse outside the Dickins and Jones department store in Regent Street in 1960

But Eric's second period with LEC Refrigeration was not without incident. In 1960, while creating a new Spring window display for the LEC showroom at 217 Regent Street (today the premises of Hobbs ladies fashion store) he heard a thunderous crash and screams from the street outside. Rushing to the door he witnessed rafts of builders' scaffolding collapse onto cars and pedestrians outside the large and prestigious Dickins and Jones department store opposite.

Grabbing his camera, which he had in a bag for the new window display, Eric immediately took photographs of the devastation he saw outside. His photos were the first taken of the amazing collapse and the wrecked vehicles and choas in the street outside.

The next day his pictures were published in almost every English newspaper, as well as on the BBC television news.

Ruby and Eric's trip to the Oberammergau Passion Play in 1960 was paid for by the fee he received for the Regent Street photos

Eric's reward from the press was an acknowledgement and a huge £200 fee – worth about £1,700 in 2021 values. He immediately used some of the cash to pay for his and Ruby's once in a lifetime holiday to Oberammergau in Germany to watch the famous passion play, which is only performed once every 10 years.

Eric and Ruby enjoying a drink out at a pub in Shoreham

Indeed, the couple spent much of the following couple of years travelling Europe – Austria, Holland, Northern Italy and Germany were favourite destinations, and staying at the Butlins Ocean Hotel in Brighton, where Eric revelled in costume parties and competitions. His corny eccentricity knew no bounds.

Chapter Seven
Swinging through the Sixties

At home in Shoreham, Eric started freelancing as a consultant electrical engineer, specialising in the rapidly growing refrigeration needs of commercial and private customers.

He was regularly driving across Sussex in his red Ford van to repair and service fridges and freezers.

One of his long-term customers was still Batten's Dairy. The dairy was housed in the old Vinery on the corner of St Mary's Road with Brunswick Road in Shoreham.

One of Eric's new commercial customers was AE Street the bakers and restaurant at 20 Brunswick Road (the premises now occupied by Truffles). They were so impressed by the refrigeration units Eric had supplied to Batten's Dairy since before the war that they ordered their first fridges from him.

Streets were an established high-class confectioner where wedding cakes, fresh cream chocolate eclairs and other celebratory cakes were made. They also catered for wedding parties with diners seated in the restaurant behind the shop.

Meanwhile, nestled in their leaded windowed cottage in Queen's Place, Eric had turned its small cellar into his own workshop and den. Here would spend hours making gifts and toys for his 10 grandchildren.

I recall for the Christmas of 1964 he made me a scale model railway station and a hillside/tunnel to go with my main present from my parents: a Hornby 00 electric train set. The funny memory about the railway station is that all the adverts on the station walls were for Craven A cigarettes.

For two of my cousins Eric made a box of flashing lights and a doll's house living room.

For a later Christmas in the 1960s Eric presented me with a gold painted tool box, stuffed full of basic tools such as a hammer, junior hacksaw and screwdrivers.

My mother recalled that he had done the same for her and her kin when they were children in the 1930s. *"He even built us a cottage in the garden, modelled our own family home,"* she said.

One abiding memory of this time was Eric's creative Christmas lights. From the beginning of December, it seemed that every socket in their house had at least two three-way adapters and from each adapter ran a stream of wires powering multi-coloured fairy lights.

And if ever there was a short-circuit or lights failed, Eric was there in an instant to repair the fault with electrical tape or silver foil from a discarded cigarette packet or even a used match to secure a loose connection.

Eric and Ruby's home at 85 Gordon Road, Shoreham

Eric and Ruby quickly established themselves as part of the Shoreham community and in July 1966 moved half a mile east to 85 Gordon Road – Eric said the move was to enjoy a larger garden. The ulterior motive was to give their small cottage in Queen's Place to their son Rod, who was working for the *Shoreham Herald* and raising a young family.

At their new home Eric wasted no time in creating a magical garden with a wishing-well, coloured paving, cultivated apple trees and his own workshop in the large dark wooden shed towards the end of the garden.

Eric enjoying a lobster salad on a day trip out in mid Sussex

With more space and a bit more spare cash Eric and Ruby were now making road trips out in their new red Austin Mini to rural mid Sussex while Eric regularly enjoyed Sundays fishing off Shoreham harbour or making weekend trips to the Mecca Social Club in Brighton.

A personal glorious memory was in May 1968 when I took part in a production of the children's stage musical *Julius Caesar Jones* at the Palace Pier Theatre in Brighton – part of the Brighton Arts Festival. As my mother had my baby sister Fiona to care for and my father was working away from home, my parents could not make it to see the finale performance.

But my grandparents promised to attend and would meet me afterwards by the pier entrance. And take me home. I was full of excitement until I realised that I had to climb in the back of my grandad's work van and fight off reels of cable, rogue plugs, fuses, bundles of wire and tools on the bumpy ride home.

Eric was at the wheel quietly puffing on a cigarette and occasionally calling out: *"Are you alright in the back there, Nic?"*

By the end of the decade, Eric and Ruby were well established in Shoreham by Sea.

They were regulars at the Crabtree, The Ferry Inn, The Marlipins and the Burrell and Buckingham Arms. Such was Ruby's weakness for a Gin and Dubonnet and Eric's love for a half pint of IPA beer that they were familiar and well-known members of the Shoreham community.

But their lives were much more than just a sandwich and a drink in the local pubs.

Ruby was already a member of the WVS (Women's Voluntary Service), established in 1938 to support the largely male ARP wardens.

In 1966 the WVS incorporated its appointment to the Crown and became the WRVS (Women's Royal Voluntary Service). It was around this time that Eric joined his wife to help organise events for the volunteers in and around Shoreham. And in doing so he made the WRVS stall at the Shoreham summer fete on Ham Road something never to be missed!

In 1969, he advertised – much to the shock of many members of the local WRVS – *"Come to this year's fete and see the Shoreham Stripper"*. His advert was so controversial that the *Shoreham Herald* refused to run it!

Then on the day of the fete more details of his one-man event emerged. For sixpence anyone could enter his home made What the Butler Saw type booth and look through a peephole to see the Shoreham Stripper. And dozens of visitors did just that, earning several pounds for WRVS funds.

Oh, and what exactly did they see?

A piece of old wallpaper with a handyman's paint stripper!

In retrospect this event evokes surreal humour and real pathos, as little did Eric know that his real father had been a butler!

Eric's arrival at the 1971 Shoreham fete as the Cadbury's Milk Tray Man wasn't quite this spectacular

Two years later Eric almost surpassed that triumph when he advertised for the 1971 fete: *"This year's surprise guest is the Cadbury's Milk Tray Man"*

The Milk Tray Man character was hugely topical and since 1968 had played on a string of primetime TV commercials by actor Gary Myers as a James Bond type action hero dressed all in black delivering a box of Cadbury's Milk Tray chocolates to a mysterious female recipient.

Readers can imagine the surprise and laughter when on the day of the fete Shoreham's own Milk Tray Man was revealed as 67-year-old Eric complete with bulging beer belly in a black polo neck sweater and trousers with black dyed hair while holding a huge 2 shillings (10p) bar of Cadbury's Dairy Milk chocolate!

Chapter Eight
The Autumn of their Lives

Following his retirement and a state pension in 1969, Eric took on a series of pocket money jobs including night security officer at Midland Bank in East Street, barman at the Swiss Cottage pub on Old Shoreham Road and for two years Bar Steward at the British Legion club in Buckingham Road.

He was a familiar sight pedalling back and forth up Gordon Road to those jobs on his rickety old black police bicycle, usually with a lit Craven A cigarette trailing from the corner of his mouth - although retirement had forced him to cut down from chain smoking 60 a day to just 40 a day.

Eric relaxing in retirement

Since 1966, and throughout their time at 85 Gordon Road, the old wooden shed in the garden had replaced the Queens Place cellar and become Eric's workspace and sanctuary.

Initially he converted and added to the shed to create an aviary to keep and breed budgerigars. Soon the space was an array of blue and green tweeting birds and newly hatching eggs.

But after two successive cold winters the ever-active Eric decided to swap his hobby for something more sedentary. He reconverted the shed into an art studio. Starting literally from scratch and armed with a few self-help books, brushes and an array of oil paints and a palette knife, Eric taught himself to paint.

Soon he was cutting his own canvasses from sheets of hardboard and turning out some basic but praise-worthy landscape paintings. Each creation was drawn from a familiar place or a photo from a magazine. And as time and practice passed his paintings improved immeasurably. Soon they were adorning the walls of the house and being given to friends and family… and even sold for a few shillings at WRVS events.

Sadly, all these years later only a few of his masterpieces remain.

Eric's other hobby of writing poetry continued unabated. His verses were on a diverse range of subjects from road tax and circus bears to Poppy Day and modern life.

Often Ruby was kept awake by the clattering of the Imperial typewriter in the dining room, before a breathless Eric would emerge at 2 or 3am with the words: *"Hey Rube, what do you think of this?"* before reading her his latest poem.

And his poetry found new legs being published regularly in the local Shoreham Herald – where the moniker EC Pounsett was a regular sight - or being read aloud on BBC Radio Brighton and even one appearance on Southern TV.

In 1969, newly retired Eric won his first proper poetry competition but was modest about his writing.

The *Shoreham Herald* at the time reported his success: *A poet with a corny sense of humour is how Eric Pounsett of Gordon Road sees himself. But it is a very modest description of 67-year-old Mr Pounsett, whose poetic career is far from being run-of-the-mill and even further from being corny.*

Mr Pounsett has no great opinion of his work. In fact, he thinks there is room for a lot of improvement. But others like it so much that he has already achieved a measure of success, most recently winning a poetry contest via BBC Radio Brighton.

Although Eric had been writing poems all of his life, he had only taken to it seriously two years earlier when he retired as a refrigeration engineer.

"I found I was bored and had to so something," he told the Shoreham Herald. "I started with humorous verse, quite corny really, then I got into more sentimental stuff."

Derrick's no fuel

(A reader's poem).

We raise our hats to Derrick Frost,
Who, seeing what oil shortage to the country
would cost.
Decided not to sit around and debate,
But flew off to the source of supply—Kuwait.
This approach to the problem was quite
unique,
In fact you will agree was far from meek.
While ministers did dilly and dally,
Derrick with the oil sheiks was getting pally.
With this initiative and a little toil,
Who knows our Derrick he may strike oil!
In any case, throughout the nation,
He's earned from us all, our admiration.
E. C. Pounsett, 85 Gordon Road, Shoreham.

One of Eric's poems published in the *Shoreham Herald*

The newspaper continued: *As the months went by Mr Pounsett began to feel more deeply involved with what he was doing.*

"I found that the crude stuff was rather a waste of time," he said. "Although people laughed, I felt I hadn't really done anything. Now I like the emotional poems best. They seem to be an outlet for me and those people reading them.

Before long he was confident enough to work on a poem based on his 40 years of married life and called "We Two".

At the same time he developed his skill at writing quickies, short sharp pieces on a simple theme.

Yet even now Mr Pounsett has an essentially casual approach to his poetry.

"I don't devote a lot of time to it," he says.

"I spent half an hour on it the other night waiting for the football to come on. Then I left it and will pick it up another time."

Pressed for a reason why he has mastered poetry so easily, Mr Pounsett is stuck for an answer. But he volunteers: "I think I have a corny sense of humour. That's probably it!"

And Eric continued writing and picking up awards including one in the national Age Concern Literary competition and a first place in the Adult Class at Hastings Festival of Poetry in 1973, where he entered his poem *Plant a Tree Year*.

The judge Rosina Pearce commented: *"The Happiness Tree is a charming idea and the strongly emphasised "Happiness Happiness – Lasting Happiness" is both novel and pleasing – do go on planting".*

Eric and Ruby begin taking it easy yin later life

Eric continued writing poetry and had over 50 poems published in the West Sussex Association for the Elderly magazine. He also received personally signed letters from Mary Wilson, the wife of Prime Minister Harold Wilson; Conservative Party leader Margaret Thatcher and members of the Royal Family thanking him for poems he had sent them.

Eric's friend and champion, the late
BBC broadcaster Charlie Chester

Eric also became firm and lifetime friends with radio presenter, writer and comedian Charlie Chester, who he first met in person in the early 1950s. Charlie, who lived in nearby Eastbourne, would regularly read out Eric's poems on his show *Sunday Soapbox* on BBC Radio 2 and write affectionate letters of thanks to him.

But Eric's greatest moment of personal recognition came in 1974, when Charlie introduced one of his verses on live radio: *"And here's another poem from my friend Eric Pounsett, or Mr Shoreham as I like to call him."*

Chapter Nine
Death is Not the End

Eric and Ruby had ridden a roller coaster of good and bad times during their 50 years of marriage and sadly there were more bad times ahead of them.

Not only were they now short of money, but Eric's smoking had finally caught up with his health.

He started suffering with chronic back pain, that even made riding his bike difficult. Plus a wheezing cough which had characterized his later years had got worse.

In 1976 he was diagnosed with Paget's Disease – painful weaking of the bones and stiffening of the joints. It is often associated with osteoporosis, hypercalcemia and sometimes with bone cancer. In addition, his doctor also diagnosed that Eric had emphysema, a chronic hardening of the lungs often caused by smoking.

There was no cure for either disease, but there were treatments. For the Paget's Disease Eric was given injections of the drug Calsynar and Calcitonin.

Calcitonin is a unique thyroid hormone. While doctors know what it does, they do not understand why we have it, and a few nasty symptoms occur if levels are high or low.

But the biggest blow to Eric was when his doctor told him he would have to stop smoking or his emphysema would kill him.

Eric said at the time: *"When I was a boy, everyone smoked. Even my mother smoked up to 30 a day until the day she died aged 94.*

"No-one knew cigarettes were bad for your health. Cork tipped Craven A, my cigarette of choice, were even marketed as "will not affect your throat" and help make breathing easier."

It was only in the 1960s that the British public began to be told that smoking was seriously harmful to health.

So, Eric was also prescribed a long-acting bronchodilator preparation Nethaprin Dospan to ease his breathing and help suppress his cough and later Phyllocontin to ease his bronchial tracts.

Eric also took the doctor's advice and after 60 years quit smoking.

The lifestyle change had two immediate impacts on him: he began chewing matches and became increasingly bad tempered and at times clearly depressed.

For a man who had never stopped working or creating this must have been a particularly hard time for him.

Ruby and Eric (far right) with other residents outside their new home at Tollbridge House in Connaught Avenue, Shoreham in 1978

Life was slowing down for both Ruby and Eric and in 1978 they took advice from their children and moved to a sheltered flat in the newly built Tollbridge House in Connaught Avenue near the River Adur. The new place was on a single level and next door to both the Amsterdam Inn and across the road from the Red Lion pub. It seemed an ideal move and location.

But life was about to play another few nasty tricks.

In 1976 Eric had been prescribed Doriden to alleviate the insomnia which was draining him of all energy. Little was known about Doriden in 1978 or its contraindications or side-effects.

Doriden was the brand name of Glutethimide, a hypnotic sedative that was introduced by Ciba in 1954 as a supposedly safe alternative to barbiturates to treat insomnia. However, it was clear that glutethimide was just as likely to cause addiction and cause violent withdrawal symptoms.

And by the time his GP ditched Doriden in September 1978 and replaced it with the drug Lentimol to treat the anxiety which had triggered Eric's insomnia - also caused largely by his back pain and his inability to smoke a soothing cigarette – Eric was experiencing some of the worst withdrawal symptoms imaginable with hallucinations and erratic, almost paranoid, behaviour.

Then matters became more serious and immediate when following a chest x-ray Eric and Ruby were told that the radiologists had detected a shadow in his right lung and that it was probably cancer.

In the early spring of 1979 Eric suffered a series of psychotic attacks and began to lose focus on where he was and what was happening. On one occasion he moved their household telephone into the broom cupboard, because he explained: *"They won't be able to hear what we are saying."*

Matters came to a head one afternoon when Ruby returned from a shopping trip to find her loving husband had taken a saw from his tool box and sawn their dining table in half.

It was done he said so he could bolt each half to opposite walls in their living room and they could *"eat apart"* so Ruby wouldn't catch the disease that was killing him.

What was happening to Eric's conscious and unconscious mind was truly tragic.

After several consultations and an enforced stay in the local Southlands Hospital, in March 1979, for a medical condition, Eric was later transferred to Graylingwell psychiatric hospital in Chichester.

Here the doctors could monitor the drugs they were giving him as well as treating the cancer in his lung which had progressed and spread quite quickly.

Everyone knew that Eric didn't have long to live but two bright moments remain of his later days.

He was told he could smoke again and the utter joy on his face when he lit up his first Craven A cigarette for more than 18 months was a scene to behold.

Then one day the ward sister asked my mum Jacqueline to come into her office for a quiet word.

"As you can imagine, Jackie, we get all sorts of patients in here. Your dad is doing quite well, all things considered, but I am still a little worried about his mental health," she said.

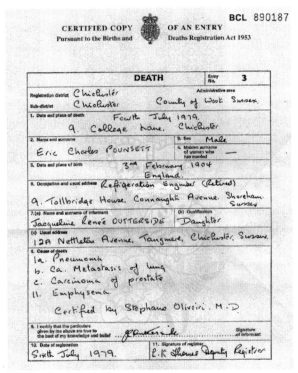

Eric's death certificate

"Twice our staff have found him in the toilet cubicles writing poetry on the toilet rolls!"

My mum roared with laughter and replied: *"He's always done that, even when we were kids."*

After being provided with writing paper and a pen Eric continued to write poems and one of his finest was titled *Country House Graylingwell*.

A few weeks later Eric died peacefully in his hospital bed at 4pm on Wednesday 4th July 1979 from breathing complications caused by pneumonia, lung cancer and emphysema.

Unlike the day of his birth, the weather on the day he died was warm and sunny.

He spent his last day surrounded by his four children, three grandchildren and his loving wife Ruby.

However, in one final cruel twist, it was only when his death certificate was issued that his family discovered the lung cancer had not been caused by Eric's chain smoking – although the emphysema had! The cancer in his lung was in fact a secondary metastasis from prostate cancer – a hidden illness that none of Eric's children were previously aware of.

Eric and Ruby's memorial stone

A service of remembrance was held at St Nicolas Church in Shoreham – just a few hundred yards from his home at Tollbridge

House and his body was cremated at Chichester Crematorium on Monday 9th July.

The *Shoreham Herald* ran a fabulous obituary to him under the simple headline of *Death of Award Winning Poet* – pictured below.

Ruby continued living at Tollbridge House before succumbing to a stroke on the steps of her home on 30th April 1984. She died later that same day in Worthing Hospital.

Both Eric and Ruby are remembered with a memorial stone in the churchyard of St Mary De Haura in Shoreham.

ERIC CHARLES POUNSETT
1904-1979
THE POETRY

Knock Upon a Door

Somewhere near to where you live, is there a lonely soul?
Maybe sitting sadly, too weak to take a stroll
So alone I this world of ours, and for them no one to care
Have you ever thought of them, or did you forget they were there?

Don't you think it would be nice, for us to lend a hand?
Just put yourself in their place and try to understand
How would you feel if someone cared and knocked on your door?
And by that act of kindness showed you were not alone anymore.

Just think what it would mean to be asked *"How do you feel?"*
And someone cared whether they had had a meal
It would not cost very much, if only we would try
To show a little kindness before their day passed by.

So why not go and look for them, you'll find life so worthwhile.
When upon an aged and lonely face you suddenly see a loving smile
Be a Good Samaritan, knock upon a door and see it open wide
And God above will be pleased, just to know that you tried.

The Bear Truth

The night the circus came to town
For fog you could not see
It was while the showmen were pitching the tent
A Grizzly Bear broke free
For hours they tried to find it
In fog as black as ink
Then someone said "I've had enough
Let's go and have a drink"
Now into the same bar came a lady
You know the kind I mean
She said to her friend who was sitting there
"I haven't earned a bean.
I've walked the streets since half past six
It's been a lousy day
The only customer was a dirty old man
In a big fur coat
And he didn't even pay."

Good Old Days

Do you often think back to those good old days in the Kings Road
Chelsea and Arthur Street?
There was always a good laugh waiting when at 67 we used to meet
Do you remember the tap, tap, tap on the floor and *"What's the
time?"* old gran would call?
"Half of cheese and a quarter of brawn" someone downstairs would bawl
"Is it as late as that?" would come the reply and what Harry said I
cannot repeat
As he went up and down the basement stairs cursing his poor old
feet
He'd come in from the scullery and in his hand he'd be holding a
jug
"I'll pop up and get your bitter now Liz" he'd say, old Harry was no mug
Do you remember those steak and kidney puds that mum boiled in
a cloth in the copper?
And do you remember the time dad killed a chicken and cut off its
head with a chopper?
Talking of birds do you remember *"Good night duck"* to some it
sounded strange
I'd say *"Good night duck"* a dozen times, Harry would shout *"Let's
have chicken for a change"*
And that door mat that could tell quite a story and Jack Johnson's
plaque that hung on the wall
Both saw some queer sights on some of those nights that I now
blush to recall
Do you remember Rob and his dirty tales and Alec with his kick on
your shin?
And the way Rob teased Betty and Vera and burst all their balloons
with a pin
Do you remember Mrs Hendra and Peeping Tom, and George who
said his father was the King?
And what about man hater Miss Fitzroy, I think a man once showed
her his thing
Do you remember the day I was married and passed out one over
the eight?

Ciss brought me up a tea on the settee and I kissed her and said
"Sorry mate"
Do you remember they once had a collie a ruddy great brute of a
dog
When you went up the garden for a quickie, it wouldn't let you out
of the bog
Well that's enough remembering but if you feel like giving me a treat
You can buy me number 67 for £40,000 but now it's called 67 Dove
House Street.

A Fair Cop

I was only going to cross the road
So I stood on the curb a tick
Then a policeman tapped me on the arm
It made me feel quite sick
The copper said: *"Allo, allo*
I want a word with you
I see your road tax has run out
It's two months overdue
I shall want to see your licence
You know you can't park here
And let's have a look at your insurance
What's this.. do I smell beer?
Just blow hard into this here bag
And I will need a sample too
No wonder we have accidents
With blokes around like you"
I listened to him patiently
And he wouldn't let me talk
You see I have no car, I cannot drive
I was only going for a walk
When at last he listened
And slowly off he went
He muttered that he would change the charge
To loitering with intent
My case comes up next Monday
I think I'll be better off by far
If to being drunk I plead guilty
And buy myself a car.

None So Blind

Has the British workman gone quite mad?
Wasn't he satisfied with what he had?
Not long ago prosperity loomed
But he had to be greedy and now it's doomed
Then the cost of living began to rise
"More money, more money!" were his greedy cries
Surely he's bright enough to know
Wage increases make costs upward go
So once again he could not cope
And another rise was demanded
Man is a dope
If only he'd stop and make deduction
Then he'd see he was creating his own destruction
Oh man, Oh man! You are a jerk
You'll strike yourself out of work!

Don't Say a Word if I Tell You

I just cannot stand scandal mongers
All the titbits you tell they repeat
You tell them it was told in confidence
And they tell the whole bloody street
Take that Mrs Scragg from over the road
She who peeps round the edge of her curtain
My wife was out when the insurance man called
She spread the rumour I was at it for certain
She's a nice one to talk I can tell you
But her six-month-old kid makes you think
No wonder her lodger's called Randy
Her old man's been two years in the clink
There's her sister Alice from up number nine
And who is it that puts her in the club?
Her last two kids were not like her old man
They're both ginger like Bert up the pub
Why is it they spread all these rumours
They spoil all the fun of a chat
You go tell a friend something spicy
And they say *"Yes Mrs Brown told me that"*
Why do they repeat all that you tell them?
I can't stand scandal mongers, I've tried
But how can you keep all you hear to yourself
When you must to someone confide.

To Each His Own

What in life is man looking for
A phantom pot of gold
Man must learn that contentment
Cannot be bought or sold
The greatest gift that man can have
Was given him at birth
If only he will use it well
He will realise what it is worth
This gift was innocence and love
And a life in which to use them
The choice is his and only his
To cherish or abuse them
If he can learn to value love
Both given or received
And recognise all right from wrong
He'll never be deceived
Whatever others' actions
If he can play the game
And by his heart be guided
Then he need never have any shame.

Silver Jubilee

God bless your gracious majesty
You made us feel so proud
When we saw you on your walkabout
Amidst that loyal crowd
We watched your celebration journey
From the Palace to St Pauls
While the nation showed their love for you
By their cheering and applause
We heard the thanksgiving service
We too had prayers to give
On this your Silver Jubilee day
We prayed that long may you live
We saw you at the Guildhall
We heard your speech with pride
For we knew the world was listening
And we all felt good inside
Finally on the palace balcony
With your family you were seen
So much the multitude did say
When they called *"We want the Queen"*
When the children of the future
Read in history of this story
They too will walk with heads held high
In this land of hope and glory

When Jesus Called

When Jesus called I tried to make amends
For wrongs I'd done to all my friends
I prayed forgiveness for sins past
And hope their memory would not last
For now I'm changed and enthralled
By what I heard when Jesus called

When Jesus called my fears soon fled
His burning words my courage bred
And in the Heavens I could see
The Holy cross which beckoned me
My errant ways I was appalled
But I feel cleansed now since Jesus called

When Jesus called I did spy
His Holy presence in the sky
Now as I near my journey's end
I know him for a faithful friend
His radiant smile holds me enthralled
I'm glad I was home when Jesus called.

All Men are Adam

When man was a boy he had no time at all
For the girls in the playground at school
He would chase, tease and torment them
And give their hair a pull

But at 14 he started to notice and whistled
And the girls would look silly and coy
He would give on a sweet or an apple
If he wanted to be her boy

At 16 he would choose one girl special
And if she encouraged his advances
He'd dress up like a dog's dinner
And take her to the pictures or dances

At 18 he would take a girl out to dine
And keep her up half the night
He would then take her home for a coffee
And what happened next... yes you're right

Now for that young man the love bug would bite
And a girl he would marry for sure
He would promise to love until death us do part
And to sow his wild oats never more

From now on that young man he was settled
And with life he now had his fill
He might even bring up a family
Either that or she'd go on the Pill

Eventually comes the time of retirement
And he meets the cruellest of fate
He's got the time to fancy every young girl
But now it's too ruddy late.

An Old Man Cried

Should you ask me why an old man cried
Just because a blackbird died?
A story to you I would unfold
I think you would understand when told
This bird was so special, you see
And the old man, that was me
Each year outside my window he would sing
Telling me cheer up old man, it is spring
Into my garden I would take my chair
And my blackbird would be waiting there
And as I sat beneath my tree
My blackbird he would sing to me
In trust he'd fly down to me feet
As I sprinkled crumbs for him to eat
He'd give a call then patiently wait
And down would come my blackbird's mate
As time went by my garden I would attend
And those blackbirds their time to spend
As they did each year deciding where best
In my garden where to build their nest
Their eggs would hatch and their young take wing
As my blackbird he continued to sing
But God thought best, as is his way
Now in my garden there is no song today
For one night a cat attacked
And my blackbird died
And in this old man's heart
Oh yes, I cried.

Peace on Earth

Christmas the time for carol singing
Midnight Mass and church bells ringing
Generous hearts and smiling faces
And showing how good the human race is

Making sure their prayers are said
We tuck our children up warm in bed
So much pleasure we get in preparation
For pleasure giving is our vacation

To all our friends our presents sent
Little caring what we've spent
Happiness is overflowing
Kindness to everyone we are showing

But it takes Christmas for us to find
That real happiness is in the mind
For out of the hearts of every being
Comes this goodness well worth seeing

If all the year was Christmas
And every day we were all kind
Peace and happiness would prevail
And Heaven on Earth we'd find.

Lorry Driver Jack

There's a tale going round town about lorry driver Jack
He took a truck up to London and broke down coming back
It was after 12 o'clock at night and miles from anywhere
Poor Jack would have to stay all night and there was no-one around
to care
Now, the only place for him to sleep was the tail-board of his truck
So he wrapped himself in an old tarpaulin and curse his flippin' luck
He had only just dozed off to sleep when someone touched him on
the arm
And standing by his tail-board was a gorgeous girl oozing charm
To Jack she was a winsome sight as she said: *"Don't think me bold
But my good man you can't sleep there all night
You'll catch a death of cold!"*
She gently took Jack by the hand and led him to her car
Then said: *"You come home and sleep with me, it isn't very far."*
When they arrived she opened the door and gave Jack a lingering
kiss
Then poured a double brandy out and said: *"Here, you drink this."*
As she led him to her bedroom she whispered in his ear:
"Hurry take your clothes off, I'll be with you soon my dear."
She started removing all her clothes and displaying her feminine
charm
When Jack fell off the tail-board and broke his bloody arm.

Called to the Bar

If you want to know people as they really are
Then try working behind a licensed bar
If they come with a pleasant greeting
Soon upon a bar stool they'll be seating
They tell you of all their financial tricks
Up in town from nine till six
They talk of their shares in oil or tin
As they sip elegantly their one pink gin
In comes a pal and its *"Hello old chap"*
Now begins the clappity clap
You stand and listen to all their bull
Wondering which thinks the other a fool?
Soon the doubles start to flow
And they boast to each other of all they know
Eventually they're on to rum and coke
Each tells the other a dirty joke
Their laughing now is not subdued
And the stories told are extremely rude
There comes the time when truly stowed
The call goes up *"One for the road"*
Three or four times this call is repeated
Till in an argument they are over-heated
Now to me this always is a joke
The financial wizard finds he's broke
Whispers to you *"I say Sid*
Could you lend a chap a quid?
Afraid I haven't got a cheque"
Too late he's out… he's hit the deck
His boozing pal doesn't want to know
Dives for the door, decides he must go
Oh well, tomorrow night it will be the same
A barman's life is never tame.

Slow Me Down Lord

Slow me down Lord
Ease the pounding of my heart
By the quieting of my mind
Steady my hurried pace
With a vision of the eternal reach of time
Amid the confusion of my day
Give me the calmness of the hills
Break the tension of my nerves and muscles
With the music of the singing streams
Help me know the magical restoration of sleep
Teach me the art of taking minute vacations
And time to look at a flower or chat to a friend
To pat a dog or recall a few lines from a book
Let me look up into the towering oak
And that it grew great and strong
Because it grew slowly and well
Inspire me to send my own roots
Deep into the soil of life
That I may grow towards the stars of my destiny.

A Time to Remember

They took the spade from out of his hand
And gave to him a gun
You're not a gardener now, they said
You're going to fight against the Hun.

They sent him out across the sea
And told him: *"shoot to kill"*
You are fighting for your country, son
Now he's lying out there still.

A "War to end all wars" they said
And so many lives they gave
So you and I can live in peace
And their reward was just a grave.

Now that was many years ago
So who does still care?
That someone's father or someone's son
For us is lying there.

They built for him a Cenotaph
And we a promise made
So we do not forget when poppies bloom
The price for peace he paid.

The time has come for remembering
All wars through ages past
And all the sacrifices made
That brought no peace to last.

He could have been your father
Never let it be your son
A *"War to end all wars"* they said
Now it's up to you my son.

A Good Buy

In the market was a stall holder
Selling ladies' wear
He was offering what he called Magic Knickers
At just two pounds a pair
But they were not selling very well
He had only sold but one
When a lady held her knickers above her head
And shouted "Hey you, I've been done"
But the store holder was not troubled
For him this was not rare
He replied "I told you they were magic
Who's the next one for a pair?"

Point Taken

Oh please be careful how you point that hypodermic
And honestly my name is not Ben Doon
I know the drugs you are using are expensive
And that I have the richest bum in town

Each time you jab, it's me who gets the needle
And I know it's costing £17 a go
I know you are making sure I get the dosage
But do you have to stick it in so low?

Some people when they get gifts of money
Put it in the bank, well that's just fine
Three times a week you make a £17 deposit
In my posterior, and I just sit on mine

There's no mistake my rear is something special
And you may think its funny, but it's not
I know I am sitting on a gold mine
But it's hard to lower my trousers and show my bot

So when next you use that hypodermic
And stick in the needle to the hilt
When the drug begins to flow, I will tell you where to go
And you can stick your needle up your kilt

The Generation Barrier

If only those aching hearts of our could make you understand
If only in our darkness we could reach out and find your hand
Never cane our words convey our feelings deep for you
We try, but there's a barrier and some-how we can't get through

You are our flesh and blood, you for whom we live
If only we could reach you, there's so much we want to give
So many things have happened that on us have left their mark
We try so hard to reach the light, but cannot penetrate the dark

Our words get locked inside us, so much there is to say
No longer do you hear our voice, from us you've gone away
Since we do fail so utterly to make you understand
We pray that you might feel for us and let us find your hand

Help us sons to find the words, help us to translate
Help us bridge that barrier, for us it's getting late

Remember we your fathers wallowed in the mire
For a better world for our sons, for that we did aspire
But we built a barrier and now the years they do divide
We could still understand and help, if only we both tried.

Memory Lane

Do you remember when you were young
The things on which your happiness hung?
Those wonderful things now in memory lane
The things we shall never see again.

Do you remember the sweets in a farthing bag
And the aspidistra mum got for a bundle of rags?
In a bran tub you could dive your hand
And on the way home watch a one-man band

You had hokey pokey penny a lump
And bought some beans that used to jump
Do you remember Tony and his performing bear
And the organ grinder with his monkey there

Did you go for a ride on a horse drawn brake
Or at the penny bazaar buy a toy German make?
Did you buy roast chestnuts at a penny a bag
And warm your cold hands on a tin of burnt rag?

On Sundays the crumpet man rang his bell
The watercress and winkle man called as well
We used to have Blakeys on our boots and shoes
Dad only paid a ha'penny for his Evening News

The lamplighter lit street gas lights with a pole
A man out of work received no dole
But you could get mother's ruin at tuppence a gill
And the girls in those days were not on the Pill

At the pictures they gave you a bag of sweets
Do you remember the iced buns at Sunday School treats
The milkman called at the door with his milk in a pail
And dad always stuck a hot poker in mum's old ale

Did you ever get a wallop from a policeman's rolled cape
Did you but locust bean or suck liquorice tape?
Well I guess that you did and remember like me
All these wonderful things that we'll never more see.

Keep off the Grass

Adur District Council was feeling jolly
And a new housing scheme was its folly
There was quite a lot of money spent
On a sheltered housing development
Tollbridge House came into being
And soon another house we will be seeing
The residents 60 to 90 years old
Have central heating and do not feel cold
The nine flat criteria was quite pleasing
But the landscaping is it out of season?
Soon Tollbridge House you will not see
For tall grass now grows where shrubs should be
Two residents coming in late got lost
In an area where grass seed was tossed
At the introduction of the scheme
It was clearly stated
Extravagant landscaping was contemplated
Now nine months have passed and the grass still grows
How long, how long, God only knows
Should the council my observations read
They can find me first right of the Groundsel weed
The Dandelions they are not too bad
But we old buggers wish some lawn we had
Please do not think I am mickey taking
But tell me what day we will help with the haymaking
A word to locals as Tollbridge House you pass
Please, oh please keep off our grass.

Not Fully Covered

My body is in a wretched state its due for an MOT
I'm sure my engine is wearing out, it's not like it used to be
My valves have started wheezing, I dare not change my speed
And my clutch has started slipping, it's an overhaul I need
I am not very bright these days, my battery is running low
And my pipes are choking up, the fluid will not flow
I can hear my engine miss a stroke, and my starter is in a state
And all my incidentals I'm afraid are getting out of date
My bodywork is not too good, it's seen far better days
My skin is full of wrinkles, just like a blooming maze
My chassis is a shambles, to believe it must be seen
I am a perfect wreck; it makes you wonder where I've been
I've only had one owner, and with care I have been treated
But I must admit there have been times when I was overheated
Still I am covered by a licence, my wife holds that you see
Because she had to take me without a guarantee.

Plant a Tree

If I could have one wish come true
A Heaven on Earth there would be
For in every garden in the world
I would plant a Happiness Tree
With care and love my trees would grow
And everyone in this world would know
Happiness

If man showed some kindness
And others from his tree a cutting take
Then love would spread around this world
Like the ripples in a lake
There would be a world of peace in which to live
If man only learned to give
Happiness

So much I wish it could come true
But alas it is just a dream
For my Happiness Trees they cannot grow
While man does fight, hate and scheme
Not until we all our own trees grow
Will the world be wise and know
Happiness

Pain Killing Jab

The National Health Service
Is a boon to every woman and man
It was Ni Bevan's post war idea
And it really was quite a plan

For 28 years I've paid my stamp
Not appreciating what it was for
But I am reaping the benefit
Now I am old and poor

Paget's Disease has taken its toll
As my frame begins to crumble
But the care from the NHS I get
Makes me feel quite humble

Sometimes the pain it is so bad
I don't know whether to stand or sit
But to ease it all, into my bum
The nurse makes a quick deposit

Ouch!

Country House Graylingwell

They said I was mad
I asked them who?
They turned and shouted you!
I answered me?
They smiled and said yes
I answered oh
I am in a mess

A poem should have a punch line
A message and a moral in its line
I hope this poem has it all
And I hope they are good and kind

The day the nurses brought me in
A straight jacket they did use
When I heard that this place was Graylingwell
I knew my freedom I would lose

Oh yes this place is a nut house
Of that I have no doubt
So whatever it is I can do
I am sane, please let me out

Yes, I spent my time
And my writing was quite bad
So finally I began to think
They must all think I'm mad

Oh yes, it is I who is round the bend
That is a fact I cannot win
Now I feel so upset
That I've committed some kind of sin

By cruelty and bad manners
Some very good friends I have lost

To regain that friendship now I would give
Anything, never mind the cost

This world is such a crazy place
And only one of is sane
Should I ever get the chance
I shall not come here again

I did once have a wheelchair
But they soon took that away
I tried to explain my curiosity
But they said shut up and stay

So let's go up to Ruby's house
And have ourselves a ball
For when I ask here for a cup of tea
They say you're getting bugger all

But otherwise they treat us well
And the food is frightfully good
But if I tell you what I really think
It would be read as something very rude

A Last Prayer

Thank you Oh God for all the people who have looked after me
today
For all those who have visited
For all the letters and get-well cards
For the flowers and gifts friends have sent
I know that sleep is one of the best medicines
For both the body and the mind
Help me to sleep tonight
Into your strong hands
I place all the patients in this ward
The night staff on duty tonight
My loved ones in their homes
And myself
Consumed by my fears, my worries and my hopes
Help me to sleep
Bound by you and your promises oh Lord
Amen

Down in the low hung
Cellar
Lived a magician
A magic maker
A toy smith
A creator
Of dreams
Of schemes
And games
With screws, tape and nails
Cigarettes and wood
Poetry and paint
Misunderstood
Never talking of his sadness
Or his unknown father
I miss your eccentricity
Your gladness
Eric my wonderful
Grandfather

My own poem about my grandfather Eric written in 2004 on the 100th anniversary of his birth

Thanks and Acknowledgements

Jac Outterside
Gill Outterside
Louise Turner
Steve Bray
Jonathan Goodger
Maureen Byford
Phyllis Dunn
Peter Beatle
Hazel Robb
Martin Sculpture
Shorehambysea.com
Shoreham by Sea Facebook group
My Shoreham by Sea Facebook group
West Sussex Registry Office

Picture Credits

Time is an Ocean	Front Cover
Time is an Ocean	Page 4
The Guardian	Page 5
Time is an Ocean	Page 8
Time is an Ocean	Page 10
Public Domain	Page 11
Dover Museum	Page 13
Dover Museum	Page 15
Time is an Ocean	Page 18
Time is an Ocean	Page 19
Public Domain	Page 21
Time is an Ocean	Page 23
Public Domain	Page 24
Unknown origin	Page 25
Shorehambysea.com	Page 27
Shorehambysea.com	Page 28
Shorehambysea.com	Page 30
Time is an Ocean	Page 34
Public Domain	Page 35
Time is an Ocean	Page 36
Time is an Ocean	Page 37
Time is an Ocean	Page 41
Public Domain	Page 42
Time is an Ocean	Page 43
Time is an Ocean	Page 44
Time is an Ocean	Page 45
Time is an Ocean	Page 46
Time is an Ocean	Page 48
Time is an Ocean	Page 49
Public Domain	Page 51
Time is an Ocean	Page 52
The Shoreham Herald	Page 54
Time is an Ocean	Page 55
BBC	Page 56
Time is an Ocean	Page 58
Time is an Ocean	Page 60

Time is an Ocean	Page 61
The Shoreham Herald	Page 62
Time is an Ocean	Page 93
Time is an Ocean	Page 97
Time is an Ocean	Back Cover

About the Author

Pulling Mussels is written and edited by Nic Outterside, and published by his independent publishing house ***Time is an Ocean Publications***.

He is the son of Jacqueline Outterside – Eric Pounsett's second child.

Nic was raised in Shoreham and Portslade and attended both Victoria Road Infants School and Benfield County Primary School. He later went to Boundstone School in Lancing to study for his A'Levels, before moving to Yorkshire for an Honours degree in Humanities and a Post Graduate Certificate in Education.

Nic is an award-winning journalist and creative author, who over 36 years worked across all forms of media, including radio, magazines, newspapers, books and online.

Among more than a dozen awards to his name are *North of England Daily Journalist of the Year*, *Scottish Daily Journalist of the Year*, *Scottish Weekly Journalist of the Year* and a special award for investigative journalism.

In 1994, 53 MPs signed an Early Day Motion in the UK House of Commons praising Nic's research and writing.

In 2016 Nic was awarded an honorary doctorate in written journalism.

Pulling Mussels is his 38th published book.

Author and Editor:

The Hill - Songs and Poems of Darkness and Light
Another Hill - Songs and Poems of Love and Theft
Asian Voices
Asian Voices - the Director's Cut
Blood in the Cracks
Don't Look Down
Luminance - Words for a World Gone Wrong
Death in Grimsby
Bones
Hot Metal – Poems from the Print Room
Poets Don't Lie
Contacts
The Man's a Tart
Western Skies
Reality Cornflakes
A Moon Magnetized This Screeching Bird
The Arbitrary Fractals of an Oracle
Dissect My Fragile Brain
Sonnets
Spiced Dreams and Scented Schemes
Minotaur and Other Poems
An Alpine State of Mind
Blue Note Poems
Love Like a Rose
Under the Weight of Blue
Echoes and Stardust
Wet Socks and Dry Bones
In Pursuit of Dragonflies
An Escape to Stay
Pharmacy
Addled Petals
Hard Rain
Baker's Dozen
When the Party's Over
Pulling Mussels

Printed in Great Britain
by Amazon